# NEPENTHE RADIANT

*poems by*

# Aimee Seu

*Finishing Line Press*
Georgetown, Kentucky

# NEPENTHE RADIANT

*for my mom*

## ACKNOWLEDGMENTS

Thank you to my siblings Haelinn, Jae and Calvin.

Thank you to everyone at Finishing Line Press, I am forever grateful to you for
noticing this.

Lisa Russ Spaar, Greg Orr, Brian Teare and everyone at the University of
Virginia's Creative Writing MFA, my pantheon.

James Kimbrell, Cy Jillian Weise and everyone who I learned from at Florida
State University's Creative Writing PhD program. These poems would not exist
otherwise.

Gratitude forever to Barbara Brown and Rosemary Maurer.

Landis Grenville, Haley Laningham and Sophia Shealy, who saw me through
heaven and hell.

"Brain Activity / Moving Photograph of Girlhood" was first published in *The
Paddock Review*.

"Zaire" & "Letter of Openings and Closings" were first published in *Swamp Pink*.

"Rich Friend" was first published in *Philadelphia Stories*.


Publisher: Leah Huete de Maines
Editor: Christen Kincaid
Cover Art: Maya S. Smith, "Creature Comforts: Companions #4"
Author Photo: Aimee Seu
Cover Design: Elizabeth Maines McCleavy


Order online: www.finishinglinepress.com
            also available on amazon.com


Author inquiries and mail orders:
Finishing Line Press
PO Box 1626
Georgetown, Kentucky 40324
USA

# Contents

*O, how we entertain the angels*
*with our brief animation. O,*
*how I'll miss you when we're dead.*

—Nicole Sealey

*Come back. Even as a shadow,*
*even as a dream.*

—Euripides
(trans. Anne Carson)

## Brain Activity / Moving Photograph of Girlhood

Late in the day the dream rises back up and invades —
My brother's radiant rage, knuckles wrapped in gauze

an aurora bleeding through. The teenage body's hellscape: crown
of my head through the windshield again. Sped-up
each time, dreaded and inevitable, as if the crash site

yearns for the crash. Then stalling at the very moment
of the kiss — those wingèd incantations of shattering glass

metal warping like an orca's groan. I crawled across the highway
toward a gorgeous mirage of you, first love, leaned back in bright light
tattoos you gave yourself with the demented electric toothbrush, all there.

But it wasn't death I saw, because I rushed toward it —
woke in a stranger's bedroom, in a stranger's clothes
that, waking a second time, I know are mine. Glass marble

inside a seashell left open, trapping the gaze of an eye.
Mine was a blessed sixteenth. Ritual sow cloaked in lilies, led singing
to the knife. Love was a ray of light sent down a turning hallway

by ricochet off precisely-tilted mirrors. The adults stood way out, shin-deep—god silhouettes on a sandbar I couldn't swim to, in the rose-gold hour, in the loneliness before words worked at all. A storm churning inside me for orderless years. You know what I mean, I can tell.

The kaleidoscope's continuous bloom, someone whispers a name in your ear you won't need for years. Here comes the part

of each month when the moon is dark as a throat. Genatalian unravel of wisteria's odorous kush. North January's harsh doubled light like a cruel smile and that deja-vuic afternoon allure to cut loose

from the helpless animal body. Same old, grade school ideation. But then, a rush of heaven—virgin fugitive in my room our small grottos of sugarwater. Ornate rainforest deathtrap flowers.

Spread my legs and watch ravenous butterflies clutter the window. My hips in her hands like all things—dissolving and arriving at once.

# PART I

## Zaire

*For T. Zaire. G.*

The daytime moon
like a coin of cloud.
One moment from youth
haunting me lately—
your stretch limousine body
on the couch behind the school
auditorium, smoke encircling
you like black koi. I live so
inundated with fantasy
sometimes I can barely see
what I'm holding.
You were my brother's
only friend, so your death
is just his. But I can carry
the porch swing and your Sea World
tee shirt, its blue bleach tie-dye, you grew
gaunt beneath. Once Reese's
and gas station pizza, then a craving
for nothingness. My mom called it
your skinny year, like anything returns
to what was. We used to love
to the tell the myth of you
walking out to the car, your girlfriend
all shredded jeans and liquid hair
yelling, she picked up a 2x4 and swung,
cracked it across the back
of your head. And you were so
fucked up that you stumbled,
stood, turned and said *That's why*
*you missed, bitch!* Got in
and we drove off howling. Epic.
How from then on, we'd quote you
to the tossed lighter, the tv remote
or the fries thrown backseat
*That's why you missed, bitch!*
As if everything coming for us
would find us but lose. The echo
of your mother saying *I keep*
*looking up the street, as if*
*he'll come walking down it,*

*any minute now*...her hands
were shaking. I was standing
there dumbly, with flowers.
Your eyes never lingered, the year
of my body's embarrassing blossoming.
Looked out for me when my brother was in Juvie.
Saying *Leave her be* to the other upperclassmen.
After that, the hallways parted
for me, like how suddenly rain
halts. Then the last summer, silent
heat lightning and brown
crystals, all of us in the woods
like lost boys, gnawing
our mouths apart. I was preoccupied
with some girl and the stars
but you are there on the edges
of remembrance, a part
of the darkness, your pulse
an imperceptible beat
in that music. I forget how the night
ended, but I escaped. Someone carried
me home, protected like you
never were. Recurring dream
of you and my brother shadowboxing
in the backyard like you used to
surrounded by slow iridescent purple
snow, you fall on each other
into softness. Thick gloves and full 40's.
I'm now a part of the living's
selfish need to depict the dead
in heaven. This year, I wake
to the large hollowness
of my room around me, it feels
about right. A man in my bed
rolls over, gets close. Says *Aimee,*
*I feel so alone.* I stay quiet.
As horses dive over
high cliffs toward the ocean
and, crashed-landing,
transform into dolphins.

## Rich Friend

Hello sounded like a new language
from her mouth. Intergalactic sparkle
   of passionfruit lip gloss. Stuck her finger
   through the threads where my thighs
rubbing together, wore away my jeans.
   *New clothes much?* she smirked. Her mother looked me up
      and down in the doorway, worried. I was mesmerized
   by the kitchen pantry. Gleam of hardwood.
   In framed photographs: Gwen in black velvet riding helmet.
Gwen at art camp. Gwen on stage with other porcelain doll
   children, tip-toe in pale tulle. Moon lowered
behind her on its rope. There was a time I would've been jealous
but, seventeen now, all I wanted was to obliterate
   the vacant house of my body, glow white
under blacklights, blast my hair straight
on the highway, pierce any flesh I could pinch. To meet crushes
   late night at the scrolling gate of her cul-de-sac. Gwen, in neon makeup
and Bjorkian rags, denim that was purposefully and expensively
   ripped or frayed or bleached. I learned
      glamorous damage, felt royal
   in her clothes.
                              And she gave generously —
      purple bomber jacket with fox fur hood,
   white corduroy bellbottoms, rainbow holographic
      wallet with the silver unicorn zipper.
Even once, an antique locket, her grandparents'
   portraits inside, frowning at me, a stranger.
   Odd that she gave it away. Odd that I wore it.
   We read how Yoko won Lennon's heart & we began
writing yes all over the walls. Across the dashboard, in the bathroom stalls
   at school. Yes, yes. Our chant. I'd see one of her yes's carved
      into a desk when we were classes apart
         and burn with our girlish devotion.
   *Yes* to the tongue-ringed music video skater
rolling a blunt in slow-motion, yes all over Johnny's face
in her Cry-Baby poster, yes, on repeat, to the song that still transports me.
To the indulgently foamed push-up bras, ordering $80 of food
   on Mommy's stolen credit card, just to throw it all up —
   what we once called fun. To the roof where we sat
               to watch night collapse over everything.
   We were a spectacle

in her father's convertible, trading
seats so she could ride shotgun and pack the bowl.
Her seat tilted back as I drove,
sound system humming the leather.
Gwen, I see you clearer now: her fascination with boys
she called *troubled*, who were banned from the mall,
who her father called *shitheads*, whose fathers punched
or burned them with cigarettes. The romancing of terrible wounds.
Gwen wanted to borrow the work boots I duct taped together
when I was kicked out in the rain
*so sick, so charming.*
I still remember the mesh canopy of her princess bed,
like the room a willow makes inside.
Our den of hoarded cigarettes, bottles her parents
didn't notice disappear, hard candy, gel pens,
Adderall, packs of gum. On vacation with her family
in Bermuda, we tore pages out of the hotel bible
& burned them on the beach, dared God to curse us.
Set off fireworks and ran hand-in-hand
when the cops came. Our LSD eyes engorged
on the Grand Canyon: so willfully red
beneath the rawhide sun. Or Colorado, us half asleep in hot springs
in the snow. I just wanted to go everywhere with her
and she wanted to bring me, like a treasured stuffed animal
or a groupie, so easily-amazed. What did her parents see —
a parasite teen coaching their daughter toward risk?
Or a mangy stray their big-hearted only-child
brought home — *De-flea me, make me presentable!*
One night I asked, lying on the floor beside her bed,
both of us spun out on her mother's benzos,

*Which of us do you think will die first?*

*Definitely you*, she said.

*Definitely.* I agreed

and we fell asleep laughing.

## Ode to Jameson

*"I don't have to be anywhere."*
—Franz Wright, *Alcohol*

I have friends who can hang
when life is easy. I've had friends
come through in the clutch.
But who else both celebrates
& consoles quite like you do?
You're the middle name of winged eyeliner
the other half of a room of spinning lights
& liquified candles, my three a.m.
slow dance. Bitter but less bitter than tears
licked from a cheek, when I'm poor
you make me feel expensive. When I'm rich
you remind me where I'm from.
Aftertaste like the sting of purifying
a wound. I dab you on the gums of my soul
as it teethes. O slurred philosopher,
distortion flower fed to the oracle
at Delphi, my charlatan epiphanies.
We figure out the whole world
don't we? And forget it by morning.
I pour you on the wind.
I dress you in honey & tea & steam.
Crimson & clover, over and over.
What brutal lullaby, a magic
spell that shrinks my enemies.
My nightlight aglow in deep emerald
& foil lettering, my nightgown
of velvet heat. Dusk is
a wilderness I know by heart.
During a breakup, my brother
said *I'm here for you but I know*
*there's no one to sleep in your bed*
*every night.* Little did he know —
python nectar, dragon drool
my wretched green-eyed girlfriend
with a pursed maroon mouth.
Jameson, I've found you
& lost you a hundred times

at one party. Who minds
a stain made of unrefined gold?
Who wants to remember every
agonizing detail? *Let them wait,*
you say, & put on my favorite song.
My desire's a lit match and you
the wick wet with kerosene, the high
-pitched ringing in my head tomorrow
from the force of the blast. Yes,
you make my desire a luminous blur.
Make me lion-hearted, make my
bruises feel like a suit of armor,
like an honor. Scarab sweat,
incarnadine holy water, rain in hell.
I've had friends carry me to bed
& that's nice. But how much better
one who sleeps on the bathroom floor
beside me, equally shattered.

## Letter of Openings and Closings

*Hello* stained glass cornea,
                    *Dear* this morning's blurred edges
                    sun coming over
                            the hill of her hip. *Oh Hello,*
Elysium hips!                    *Dear* lovely haunting
        of her sable   spacious hair.
                    *Dear* thing I didn't know
                            how to dream.

    *To* the party that clothed us
in enough smoke and noise
        *To* touch. *My Dear* hot pink
            moon pouring square light
            in my window the first time
                        she slept in this room.
                    *Dear* swallowed time
before we met,
        brazen-shy wanting,
        *Dear* myself kissed —
open,            Dear hibiscus tea, my tongue
            turning red, Dear tapioca, angel food
        apricot liqueur of her,            *To Whom it May*
                    Devour, *Dear* favorite
                muscle, they say
                    the tongue heals
faster, *Dear* back seat
        sighing into
            sobering up, coming to —        to her eyes.


                    *Dear* front seat on the highway one hand
        reached across. *Attention* her ambidextrous adrenaline —
*O*, to cum with the windows down.
*To* the couch dismantled
                in some friend's lost Atlanta
living room — I want to always be
        sleeping in too small a space with you.
            *Dear* soft comforter
                            pulled over us
            like a room made of cloud.
*Finally*, my body smells
like her t-shirt,

*Dear* tinted window
and restraint, *Dear*, when we weren't speaking, the pressure
                              in the air was like just before hail.
                    *Dear* battlefield of her voice.
                              Witch burning of her
                    brow. She smiled a jean jacket sadness
                                        and all the birds
                                        took off at once.
*For the attention of* everything she witnessed
as a kid from the backseat, the heat-mirage she saw alone. *Love,*

I feel women kissing through
us who time held
apart.
                    Kneeling in the shower, all the birds took off at once,
                                        as if tied by string.
                    *Dear* I'll find you at the concert, at low
                                        tide, and at the airport
                    in the afterlife. Yours Truly, this danger
                    moved deliberately into
because someday we'll die —


                                        X O
                    (I climb up to her mind's treehouse
                    spangled by the shadows of leaves.)
          *As* ever,
                    our bodies pressed like two branches
                              of a diverted river
                              flowing back into one.
                              *P.S.* Heaven
                              will be listening to you read
                    aloud, on a blanket awash in sunshine (green slope,
                              hot afternoon, where I'm always.)
*Sincerely,*
in the whisper-licked ear, *From*
when your name in my mouth first felt
like an ember
          in wind.
                    No one saw this forest fire
                    coming, *Always, again soon,*
                              *Your Unalterable*

girl drunk on drives
before dawn, our ex-boyfriends
hunting us. Girldrunk on your taste
in secret, wide open fields. *Fervently*
each one-more-time, until
we're a drooling mess of quartz
limbs, pretty corpse of each small
death's levitation. *Love*
myself enough to give me this. *Affectionately,*
disappearing into her pupil's black void.

# PART II

## October

Beside the highway cows in blue rain.
I knew my soulmate snorting lines
off my collarbone, the center console.
Telling youth in small glimpses: metal
lash of her father's belt, second-story
jump from a window to escape. We fly
90 to make it to the amusement park
before close. Speed unlocks her: muted
child witness of an unnamed half-
sister's umbilical noose, swears
she'll never go willingly into
a hospital again. Florida sky
swirling enormous above us
like a tortured mind, shredded gauze
of airplane trails. A word I hold
on my tongue these months: *E—qui
—ðis—tant*, sounds like horses, earth,
then metal beaten to a thin gleam.

I kept the sheets with her cum
and period blood on my bed, sucking
a lollipop and staring at them, long
after, laying my new blood there against
like those places where saltwater
meets inland stream. Like her open
mouth in mine, like her wet
pressed and rocking like waves
against mine. Invisible to the naked
eye—where one water ends and another
begins, the rare life that can only exist
in the conditions of such collision. My tongue
tangled in the climbing light of a kelp forest.
Her fingers slow diving each cuddling reef
of my body. How we found each other
faster in the dark.

       A., the before-dawns
we woke in your room in your mother's house
and crept out to drive, sun greyly rising,
to the beaches, and you drank ashed-in
warm beer from the night before and I

lit a gold Spirit and hung my bare feet
out the window watching the wires
rise, crest, fall like a conductor's wand
and day yellowed like a spell
you parked, kissed me hard, parted
and I'd brush my teeth in the big stall
of the Walgreens bathroom and gaze
at myself in the mirror where someone
jaggedly knifed *me + you 4ever*, for once
I found myself beautiful, protected by your love.
It is no small thing for me to wake and want
to be alive. And I'd buy a gallon, cans of bad
white wine, walk the block to the beach,
stretch leonine in the sun, record every
way you'd touched me the night before
with red pen in my diary, pages gilded
and falling apart, sitting on the ragged towel
balled up in my backpack all summer to sleep
beneath on the Greyhound away from you, weeping
among the junkies, each enclosed, shivering
in our own comedowns. In the weeks after we
ended someone said *What is heartbreak*
*but chemical withdrawal from love?*

But at the sunrise coast: a tryptic of pelicans
gliding the airways, and I'd get in the ocean
even in rain, when secretly, it's most lovely
because the air, threaded silver,
becomes cold but the water remains warm
and as people fled, umbrellas closing
hurriedly like wounded hearts, I'd slide in and down
to lay on the rippled ocean floor: green
cathedral's glass vaults shifting above me,
the muffled patter. Cursive shadows
of skates and jellyfish distantly illumined
by lightning like wicked, joyous, unshackled
dreams. Knowing Florida's July storms pass
quickly, and later I'd run to her in the street
her black cook coat unbuttoned, the slash
and labyrinth of a metal band's lettering

across her tidepool chest on the hoodie beneath,
(because even in summer, she's always cold)
dreads drawn back, austere architecture
of her face interrupted, momentarily
by the smile I loved best, that somehow survived
childhood unchanged, returning now
for me. And I'd kiss her and kiss her.
Like waking up thirsty, I drank her.
Her red umber skin against my tiger's eye
tan, my toes on her skateboarding shoes,
her cello-low hello. Forearm's raised marks
like days tallied on a wall in confinement.
How to include her beauty and her pain
without beautifying her pain.

A., remember the recording you took
of me in the very beginning, *Annabel Lee*
in the grass with birds, tinkling windchimes
in the background, the lovers' souls whom even
deep-ocean demons after death can't divide.
Or the layered soundbite, my moaning
over the song you wrote, high-pitched sighing
saying your name, your grunge and heavy bass.
Numerous bright and shadowed nudes. The ways,
for each other, we let ourselves be captured.

But ours was a different sort of kingdom
by the sea. A., when you said your favorite
snack growing up was ketchup packets
I tried to hide my constricting chest.
I knew you didn't want my pity.
We learned love is a party that, to get into,
at least one person must believe they belong.
Could we ever get there? Ketamine flooding
my bedroom, laying interlocked with you
beneath covers, Johnny's voice slowed
to a strange drawn velvet, *I fell in
to a burning ring of fire, went down down
down, and the flames went higher,* dissociates'
sweet dissolve + oxycodone's nodding nada

*I fell for you like a child*, noticed a concentric ring
of amber-bladed daggers in your cornea
pointing inward...*and the fire went wild.*

Late nights of you screaming on facetime,
me pleading when you put cigarettes out
on your skin. My big sister, concerned
psychologist, said you reminded her of soldiers
she'd worked with, so accustomed to warzones
they couldn't completely return. *They learn
to mistrust peace.* I told her to keep her pathologies
off us. A., I only recall the bad
in shattered pieces. But I know I must.

      Still, let me turn away
to laying with the seats back
in your car parked next to the inlet
where the sailboats docked, us on lsd,
I was staring up at the windwild palms
blurred in sun, bright indigo cloudless dome
through your sunroof's glass, music loud enough
to rattle the cupholder change, you pressed a vibrator
to my wine-red lace, blew blunt smoke
in my mouth. We'd held hands in a gallery
watching Dr. Seuss and Dalí melt, trailed
by a suspicious art student, ate blue
grapes off a trespassed arbor, shared a beer
in boardwalk haze, ended up here in the height
of the visual bloom and tactile shockwaves, swirling
estuary, pouring into each other. A., each time the memory
is somehow different, a little less, a near-
imperceptible erosion, no matter how I hold
it, perhaps because I try to—some
microscopic disintegration, dust
from a butterfly's wounded wing. I'm trying
to write what only you'll understand
before we both forget, what could possibly
reach you. I don't need to understand it myself.

And for all our wildness, the quiet hours
too: bored in my room she arranged perfumes
in order of her preference, rough drummer
hands delicately placing down small bottles.
Laid her head against my chest
and said it sounded like a jellyfish
pumping towards the surface, then turned
kissed my sternum. I think it was June.

A., alone in afternoon, I conjure
your steady gaze above me, touching
myself, your pupils like polished volcanic glass,
warm always in sex, like honeycomb,
luminous, a felled tree's brown-gold rings,
your breath in my ear like time slowed
in the curl of a wave. *Nothing I can do
to my body compares to what you did.*
I try to tell you, staring off after,
seeing stars. Can you hear me?
These days I'm a black hole—
something faraway, swallowing itself,
made of loss. Every slight breeze
blows across the fresh wound of you.

Nine years with Gabriel, then two
and a half with H. Why was it you,
A.? Collapsing castle. My lost
world. Galaxy wrecked in chrysalis.
Some small justice in this
at least—love isn't a simplified
equation of languor vs. lapse.

That night, in Poe's ballad, two doomed
kids lay head-to-head, beneath fireworks
on cold sand, drug letting them down slow
the night sky's angels aflame, exploding
with jealousy, coveting us. A.,
I miss you so much I can't speak it to anyone.
These days nothing touches me.
I've been living here in the poem instead.

Where you can be suddenly beside me
like this—dimensions of your jaw
in my hands, thumbing your lower lip's
crooked scar, your smell of damp firewood
beginning to smoke, pulling my hips
towards yours. Light-warbled, glimmering
as if each moment a river rushes more quickly
between us. Must I lose this too?
Nepenthe burning away
on my tongue.

          Anayah, I've been
wearing the perfumes backwards,
saving your favorite. Small holdout
in case everything I know to be true
isn't.

You once said we were one spirit
in two bodies, finding each other again.
You knew I'd melt at that sentiment.
If so, you returned to me damaged.
I remind myself of the phone combed
through over and over, your doubled episodes
of hearing voices, misremembering
my face. Purple streetlight screaming match.
You busted your knuckles punching
the telephone pole. Like your military
-turned-pastor father took everything
out of your bedroom, even the furniture,
the Kim Althea poster, as teen punishment
and locked you in it for whole weekends
while he trashed your boyish clothes
drowned your cell—some nights your eyes
became two locked, vacant rooms.
And I was so naive, stunned by the uselessness
of all my love—how I'd thought it could undo
anything, even time. When I felt
for a shadowed flicker (trees tearing passed
on backroads, hour of your blinded rage)
that you might hurt me, I knew we had to be done.

Because I didn't mind. I heard myself think
how I'd pay that price to be with you.
That your life altering mine in any way
was a gift. Something broken in me
posed as much danger to us
as anything in you.

                    Days of colorless comedown
as she slept I stared down the length of her arm
off the bed, trying to imagine a possible future
for us but could see only a blue unfurling
lightlessness. Rolled over, kissed her face
-tattoo, baby-hairs, that memorized shoreline,
whispered adorations in her sleeping ear.
I remind myself of that sadness, concentrated
weeks of its iron weight, pounding storm I couldn't see
a few feet ahead in, how I almost killed
us both, vision underwater driving the bridge.

                    How the fall from the top
of the highest roller coaster felt
like a brief moment of peace. I clasped
her hand so tight it hurt, I know
there's nothing we can touch without, in some
small way, destroying. Even holding gently
in the mind's eye. *Remember*: her neck's
red-eyed bat tattoo and hickied thigh's
broken vessels like a universe of garnet.
*Remember*: late in the day in a dark room
ribs of light from the blinds. Opening
voiceover from the Dracula remake—
*I have crossed oceans of time to find you.*
The beauty that, by the end, will be felled
lays close in bed on the same pillow.
The sun rises and she opens her eyes
and the sun rises. A., I wouldn't mind
appearing a lunatic to this world, if privately I was lost
inside a memory of you. We stopped before our love
ruined us. This is its own kind of death.

Sitting outside the sex shop hungover
in the morning, cigs for breakfast, your hand
in a cast of torn-up tee shirt tightly tied,
I joked that we'd get married the day
I got a real job, so you could have health
insurance, meds for paranoia, fix our
fucked-up teeth. You said you'd take my last
name, because yours is your father's.
And a slave name. There are no equal
distances. Multitude pains you carry
that I will never comprehend. Forgive
my breathless attempt to collapse you and I
in every way, into one. And the unsoundable
ocean it placed between us.

                                                    A.,
the world didn't want us to meet
but we did. We will heal. I will find you
like that first night at the screamo show —
your black Skully, dreads down and bleached
gold, thick thermal in late spring. Nodding
and smiling back like we already knew.

In the morning when I'm not fully surfaced
from sleep, you arrive in the green light-lattered
place in-between. Silver-soft shelter before dawn,
that secret cove which time's racing moves around.
Leagues of stillness, the crashing so distant, we go
slow, our bodies like cool and warm currents meeting.
And you ask, like you always did, if you can
and I say, like I always did, please, please do.

**Aimee Seu** is the author of *Velvet Hounds*, winner of the 2020 Akron University Poetry Prize selected by Philip Metres. She graduated from the University of Virginia Creative Writing MFA Poetry Program in 2020 as a Poe/Faulkner Fellow where she was recipient of the 2019 Academy of American Poets Prize. Other awards she's received include the 2020 Los Angeles Review Poetry Award, the 2020 Henfield Prize for Fiction, the 2016 Academy of American Poets Prize at Temple University, the Temple University 2016 William Van Wert Award, and the Mills College Undergraduate Poetry Award. She was a finalist for the 2020 Black Warrior Poetry Prize judged by Paul Tran and a semifinalist in the 2019 New Guard Vol. IX Knightville Poetry Contest judged by Richard Blanco.

Her poetry, fiction and nonfiction have appeared or have forthcoming publications in *Poets, Ninth Letter, Pleiades, Los Angeles Review, Honey Literary, BOAAT, Redivider, Raleigh Review, Diode, Minnesota Review, Blacklist, Adroit, Harpur Palate, Philadelphia Stories, Runestone Magazine*, etc.

She attends the Florida State University Poetry PhD program.

www.ingramcontent.com/pod-product-compliance
Lightning Source LLC
Chambersburg PA
CBHW022102080426
42734CB00009B/1460